AF881136

The Companion Workbook to Trauma and Well-Being Among Legal Professionals

By

Dawn D'Amico

LCSW, PhD, CFCM

Summerland Publishing
Offices in Salt Lake City, UT and Summerland, CA
www.summerlandpublishing.com
Email: summerlandpublishing@gmail.com

© 2021 by Dawn D'Amico

First Edition.

All rights reserved. No part of this book may be reproduced or transmitted in any form or by any means, electronic or mechanical, including photocopying, recording, or by any storage or retrieval system, except in the case of brief quotations embedded in critical articles and reviews, without prior written permission by the publisher.

Although the author and publisher have made every effort to ensure the accuracy and completeness of information contained in this book, we assume no responsibility for errors, inaccuracies, omissions, or any inconsistency herein.

Printed in the United States of America.

ISBN #: 978-1-7329072-9-4

Library of Congress #2021904956

Dedication

To

Michael and Agatha

Welcome

The Companion Workbook to *Trauma and Well-Being Among Legal Professionals*

Welcome, I am so glad that you have decided to expand your knowledge and skills as you work toward greater well-being.

As we discussed in the book, *Trauma and Well-Being Among Legal Professionals*, as a legal professional you encounter a wide array of experiences, many of which are interesting, dynamic and thought provoking, and others are highly provocative, and trauma filled.

This workbook provides a series of additional tools to help counter these experiences and to improve resiliency. These tools will promote coping, quieting, grounding, and healing. Ultimately, practicing and using these tools on a regular basis will improve the quality of your work and personal life.

Please remember, we are all on this journey together, therefore let us normalize this work.

Talk about it, share it and as always, I am happy to help you. Please feel free to contact me at: lawyersatrisk.com.

Here is to our continued well-being!

Most Sincerely,

Dawn

Table of Contents

Bubble Chart (hands-on)

Take five minutes and create a bubble chart.

In each section list the following:

- The person I am closest to is…
- I am most peaceful when…
- Things that make me happy are…
- I get sad when…
- I am good at…
- My friends are…
- Things I worry about…

In the middle, place a self-portrait or represent yourself with a symbol such as a color, flower, car, etc.

Now take another moment and reflect.

What do you see in each bubble?

When we look at each bubble do you find calmness or some respite until you visit the worry bubble?

Can any individual, activity, or place help you right now, in this moment, with your worries or strengthen your coping? If yes, then plan how to engage with that individual, activity, or place today. Plan a simple phone call or text or viewing a photo of your peaceful place.

How can you spend more time engaging with people and activities that make you feel good? Do some brainstorming, place it in your calendar and make it happen.

- Praying
- Practicing mindfulness
- Calling a friend or family member

This is a jumping-off point for you. Create your own list and add it to your toolkit. Start using healthy, self-soothing behaviors.

As you use these new behaviors you will be creating new neural pathways, which help us to become more resilient.

Self-Compassion Break (hands-on)

Create a list of things that you can do for yourself that are compassionate.

Create a small box that contains items that help you to care for yourself and cope. Some people may include in their box a positive statement to remember to lighten up, a quick-cool packet to ease a headache or tension, a funky pen, bags of herbal tea or hot chocolate, a good piece of chocolate, a yo-yo to remind them to play, Silly Putty or Slime for different sensory stimulation, and essential oils or their favorite fragrance.

Keep a box at your desk or in your bag so that you can have access to it when needed.

VentArt (hands-on)

VentArt is a creative, demonstrative, and bold way to express emotions. I initially created VentArt to provide a mechanism to help reduce violence and ease trauma in schools. This technique also helps reduce violence and ease trauma with adults.

You do not need any actual artistic ability to create VentArt. VentArt allows you to express emotion in a restorative way.

Simply get a pen and paper (or any other medium) to draw, color, or paint out your feelings. You can use different paints to create large swaths of color to help show an intensity of feeling. You can use stick people to re-create real life experiences that were disturbing. You can create yourself in scenes, for instance showing yourself slaying the dragon and being the hero. (One individual drew this after feeling like he was slaying a monster dragon when he was working on a particular case.) I have had other drawings in which nausea was depicted by creating a stick figure that was throwing up with a real-life scenario in the background.

VentArt's use of color and images can be provocative and powerful and can say more than we may be able to verbalize at any given moment in time. It's also a way to communicate our feelings with others, if we chose to share. Above all, VentArt is a way for individuals to process difficult emotional experiences.

An example from my work life, when I was in the middle of working on a blended family issue and I became quite frustrated: I knew that I had release the feelings, so I drew them out. I created yellow swaths with a highlighter to represent frustration and blue marker in circles and jagged lines to represent talking in circles. When I had completed the VentArt, I felt like I had just run a fast mile. I felt better and I was able to release the emotions. VentArt helped me to move past the emotions so that I could get back to more rational thinking processes and create a solution.

Another interesting example occurred when an individual used washable paint. She showed me her work. It was full of dark purples and blues, which were very heavy and somber. However, within a few days the colors had changed, they were much lighter and calming. When the individual reflected on the painting, she said as time passed, she felt calmed too.

Compassionate Art (hands-on)

Even if we are not artists or even consider ourselves artistic, we can use color to convey our internal emotional states. Think outside of the box. Try finger paints or paint with your toes, yes, your toes.

If you are trying to create something soothing, use color that is soothing for you. I love lavender. Just looking at the color makes me feel relaxed and reflective. Use art as compassion for feeling states.

Go outside and fling some paint onto a poster board. Or paint heavy dark lines if you are sad. Get it out of you, and onto canvas or any medium. You can use recycled cardboard.

Try this tool again in a couple of days and check in with your emotional state.

Compare the two days and notice how different or similar each are. Try painting on a weekday and then on a weekend. Is there a difference? If so, what do you notice and what can you do with this information?

If you prefer, make a collage out of old magazines and newspapers. Use only words or only photographs; make it uplifting and colorful. Cutting with scissors and using glue or paste can be very relaxing and soothing. Keep your collage somewhere in sight or at least in your private sight, so that you can look at it often.

Taking It to the Street (cognitive)

Work through continuing education and professional meetings to enlarge and normalize the conversation about mental health.

Invite speakers who are known within the country and internationally to speak on these issues.

The more we talk about these issues, the more normalized the issues become and the more opportunities we have for open discussions and ultimately, action.

Create a list of ways that *you* could begin to become more educated and involved. Could you listen to a podcast, join a support group, etc.?

How could *you* get others involved? Do some additional brainstorming and see what you discover.

Productivity and Balance (hands-on)

Every now and then touch base with yourself in writing.

Create a T-chart, as we did in the book and list what you have produced in terms of work and how you are balancing your work life and your health.

Remember, work and health should not be mutually exclusive.

Are you productive, not only productive in work but are you being productive in the areas of balance and health?

Arc you acting on and fulfilling the areas of your life that keep you healthy and provide you with a sense of well-being?

If not, why not? Reevaluate and act. If yes, congratulations. Keep going.

Getting Quiet (cognitive)

Find something that calms you, that quiets your central nervous system even for just a few minutes.

Whatever you find must be healthy and not a substance: no alcohol, drugs, or food.

Some possibilities include mindfulness, meditation, prayer, Tai Chi, meditative yoga, transcendental meditation, or just sitting quietly, petting an animal or mindfully observing a plant.

If you are observing, look at the details. For example, if you are mindfully aware of a plant, look at the leaves, the texture of the leaves, and the way the veins of the plant run through the leaves.

The purpose is to notice detail. This detail quiets your mind and gives you a break from ongoing chatter and noise.

It only takes a few moments to notice things around us and get quiet.

What a relief getting quiet can be.

Candle Work (hands-on)

Candle work is a tool that I created more than twenty years ago. Although it always amazes me how simple and effective it is, it can be difficult for some people in the beginning. People always tell me "Oh, I can do that," and then get disappointed or frustrated when they cannot. But it works if you keep trying. Here is what you do:

Get a candle, go into a darkened room, and light your candle. Set a timer for just one minute. (In my experience, people who are beginners in mindfulness or mediation cannot go beyond ten seconds without having to stop.) The goal is to simply observe the candle. Notice the flame, the color of the flame, the intensity of the flame, the smell of the candle, the heat of the candle, the candle wax dripping. As you are observing the candle, you will notice thoughts coming into your mind. Maybe thoughts such as, what am I having for dinner, what do I have to do next?

When the non-candle thought comes in, imagine the thought crossing over your forehead and literally falling away from your right or left temple. Choose the right or left temple based on if you are right- or left-handed, then bring your attention back to the candle. If a repeated thought comes in, acknowledge the thought. You could say it out loud: "I recognize you, you are a reoccurring thought, and I will deal with you later." Go back to focusing on the candle. If the same thought comes back, blow out the candle and stop the exercise.

The goal is to be able to be with the candle for one minute. Be patient. If you are starting at 10 seconds, which is where most people start, it will take some time. Add time as you can and do candle work every day, it only takes one minute. The benefits are dramatic. You are creating a quiet space in your head, even if it is only for a couple of seconds in the beginning. One of my clients has moved his candle work from 10 seconds to one hour, over time. This individual's levels of anxiety and stress have dramatically decreased as he has practiced this technique. Remember, as with all things, be patient with yourself. You are worth the effort.

Flexibility versus Rigidity (cognitive)

Most successful people have plans and stick to their plans. They have day to day schedules which they maintain to meet their goals.

The task now becomes, how do you manage change?

Are you flexible, able to easily move from one task area to another? Or are you so tightly scheduled that you have anxiety or panic if your schedule needs to flex?

Try to look at changes as encouragement to learn flexibility.

We are constantly in a learning process.

We can all think of times when we have had to change quickly, how did we cope, what did we do?

What could we have done better or differently?

The more challenges that come into your schedule, the more flexible you become, so when a change occurs, you are not panicking but rather moving fluidly.

Keep in mind your must-dos to maintain health and well-being, and to-do's, they are vastly different.

We want to remain flexible, and that is part of the reason why we physically exercise: moving different muscle groups to keep us flexible. When we must be flexible in our schedule, we are learning new ways of coping with the changes and ways to remain calm in our emotional state too.

We have all heard the old statement, remain flexible, otherwise you may break.

Brainstorm ways that help you to cope with change.

Sometimes just sitting for a minute comparing your to-do list with your must-do list can be enough to formulate a plan for change.

Try it.

Self-Talk, Part 1 (cognitive)

At the end of your day, take an inventory of your self-talk.

Is it negative and criticizing?

Is it understanding and supportive?

What themes do you notice?

What kinds of self-talk take place in certain places or situations, or with specific people?

Maybe your self-talk about work is negative, your family life or personal life self-talk is positive.

What kinds of self-talk take place at certain times of day?

Maybe you notice certain times of day when you have more positive self-talk. Maybe early in the morning you have more energy and enthusiasm, or maybe later in the day you are more relaxed and positive.

Or do you notice that at certain times of the day you are grumpier or easily frustrated? Perhaps in the morning, your attempt to get out of the door frustrates you.

Or maybe those feelings coincide with mealtimes, or the drive home, or the work you take home with you.

Track yourself.

Check the themes, and name the negative feelings; grumpy, frustrated, angry, guilty, easily upset. Then find where the pattern is.

Once you discover the where, who, and how, you can begin to make a change.

Again, think small positive change.

You are frustrated as you leave home. Did you have time to eat breakfast?

Make a small change, grab a breakfast bar to take with you for the ride or walk.
Maybe the night before, have the ingredients ready for a healthy smoothie; blend and go.

Determine what, who or how, and adjust. Make it better for you.

Self-Talk, Part 2 (hands-on)

For a couple of days, create a T-chart of your negative self-talk.

On the left side of the T-chart is your negative self-talk statements.

The right side of the T-chart is the challenge or the corrective thought side.

For example:

If your negative self-talk statement is "I never have enough time to get my job done."

First, challenge that thought.

Is it really true? Probably not.

You can think of times, perhaps several times, when you complete what you set out to do.

In the challenge or corrective thought side write down the new, replacement thought: "I complete tasks. Sometimes it feels like a struggle for time, but I am a good student/legal professional and I complete my tasks."

Check:

What appears to be true? What are you creating?

If we take the example, I have committed myself to a schedule of writing all day, but I want to go for a walk while it is sunny outside. My self-talk says, you do not have the time, you planned to work all day on the book, you don't need a break, you are moving forward. A break could cause you to have difficulty refocusing when you return to the work. I challenge those thoughts and ask myself, what could be a challenge or corrective thought? Start with the first example, with the self-talk followed by truth statements:

NEGATIVE SELF TALK

1. "I never have enough time to get my job done."
2. "I don't have time to go for a walk."
3. "I planned to work all day."
4. "A break could cause me to have difficulty refocusing when I return to my work."

CORRECTIVE THOUGHTS

1. "I complete tasks. Sometimes it feels like a struggle for time, but I am a good student/legal professional."
2. "I have the same time as every other human being including those of great inventors, writers and thinkers, I can choose to take a break and a healthy walk."
3. "Yes, I planned to work all day, but I also want, and moreover need, to remain flexible. Part of working all day is still including healthy breaks."
4. "Breaks are beneficial for focus. We need breaks even when we feel like we don't in order to maintain clarity of thought and focus."

This tool allows me to take a break and go for a walk without feeling guilty or feel that I was not doing what I promised myself I would do. It will help you to do the same. Try it.

Create a Positives Notebook (hands-on)

Create a list of your positive attributes, the things that you like about yourself.

The goal is to challenge yourself to create a hundred positive attributes. You can do it. You have 100 attributes maybe you just forgot or maybe you are focusing primarily on the negative.

If you get stuck, think about compliments others have genuinely shared with you. Reflect on those compliments and see if you can accept them and include them in your list.

I can start your list for you:

- ✓ You are a good listener.
- ✓ People like you.
- ✓ You are a good conversationalist.
- ✓ You are a good friend, sister, brother, mother, father, pet owner, caretaker.

Keep adding to the list.

Poetry Process (hands-on)

Write a poem about your emotional state. This is not to share. It is just for you. Maybe you can write a short piece, such as a Haiku.

Seek out published poets. Read some classics, or poets' journals.

Read about the different emotional states people experience and share.

Remember, we all have an emotional life.

Some of the most renowned poets have suffered, survived, and thrived and their poetry lives on for generations. Many poets have processed their own feelings and experiences through their poetry.

Your poetry is only for you unless you chose to share it. Then head for the next open mic or poetry slam.

Let go on paper.

Commit (cognitive)

Commit yourself to using one tool of your choice, every day for one week.

Stay with the tool for the entire week. When we first start something new, we may feel nervous that we should be doing something else, like our work instead of taking care of ourselves.

Push through, so that you can feel the benefit of the tool.

Notice how you feel physically and emotionally.

What were you able to change in your schedule to accommodate the tool?

Be aware that you were able to be flexible and allow the new tool into your schedule.

The Nonverbal Mirror (cognitive)

When you are feeling tense, stressed, or anxious, check your reflection in a mirror.

Note where you may be holding the stress or tension in your face. Are your eyes crinkled, your brow furrowed? Are you frowning?

As you are looking in the mirror, attempt to release the muscles around your eyes and unfurrow your brow.

Can you feel the difference?

If you are frowning, bring your mouth into a neutral position and then try on a smile.

Do you notice a difference when you smile?

Now take a breath and attempt to relax all the muscles in your face.

You may appear relatively expressionless, that is OK.

The next time you notice these feelings of stress, tension, or anxiety arise, practice going back to the mirror and doing the exercise.

Eventually, you will be aware of the muscles in your face without looking in the mirror. Then you can work on relaxing the muscles and get back to a more neutral position, which can allow for a calmer state of mind.

The benefits of a calmer state of mind are clarity of thought.

Smile (cognitive)

Yes, smile.

While you are doing your work, or any time you think of the word smile, do it.

Scientists tell us that when we smile, real changes occur in our body, and we feel better.

The muscles around the mouth are providing signals to the brain. I am smiling as I write this for you.

Test it.

Try smiling.

In addition to feeling better, even for the moment, you may notice that you had been frowning, scowling, or grimacing before.

Perhaps, one of these facial expressions is your usual expression and you are not aware of it.

Try smiling during difficult times.

We do not always need to bear down and tighten up to get things accomplished. Try to remember to break the old patterns and occasionally, smile.

Beware of Transference (cognitive)

Professionals should be aware of transference and countertransference.

We all come to the table with our background, personal history, and stories, as do our clients.

Transference is when an individual transfers feelings and attitudes from an experience in their past onto a person or situation in the present. For example, a negative or even traumatic experience with an influential person, such as a school principal, may be transferred, without awareness, onto other school principals or authority figures.

Transference is acted out by everyone, and often contributes to decision-making.

We may find ourselves reacting more positively or negatively toward a particular client. Checking ourselves and checking in with our peers can help us sort out our bias, judgments, and feelings. If we recognize that we are struggling in a particular situation, we may consider passing this case to an individual who is not struggling with the particular issue.

Storytelling, Part 1 (cognitive)

Write a short story in the third person about a particularly emotionally challenging case.

Describe what it looks like and feels like for the characters in the story.

Describe ways in which the legal professionals in the story may be affected and what kinds of tools could they use to cope.

Pass these anonymous stories around to others and discuss further.

Storytelling, Part 2 (hands-on)

Write a short story about a known case that you may think of frequently.

Follow the same steps as above, describing what it looks like and feels like for the characters in the case.

Describe what it feels like for you encountering this information. (This may be the first time you have ever been asked what it feels like.)

Describe ways in which the legal professionals in the story may be impacted and what kinds of tools they could use to cope.

You might want to have a sharing event in which members of the team review and share their stories and use of coping tools.

Our Story (cognitive)

What is your story?

We have an ongoing personal dialog with ourselves. This dialog is about value and judgment and determining the next step to take. Sometimes these next steps are based on old, obsolete stories. Are you using any of these obsolete stories in your daily dialog?

What stories are historical and need to be forgotten? Where did they come from, and how old were you when these stories were created? These questions may help you to uncover old stories that are no longer needed but that still impact day to day living.

When under stress, we sometimes revert to the old narratives. They are old and no longer relevant, but we cling to them tenaciously. Watch yourself and check it. You now have new ways of behaving and being that are healthy and balanced.

This dialog is about value and judgment and determining the next step to take.
Sometimes these next steps are based on old, obsolete stories.

Are you using any of these obsolete stories in your daily dialog?

What stories are historical and need to be forgotten?

Where did they come from, and how old were you when these stories were created? These questions may help you to uncover old stories that are no longer needed but that still impact our day to day living.

When under stress, we sometimes revert to the old narratives. They are old and no longer relevant, but we cling to them tenaciously.

Watch yourself and check it. You now have new ways of behaving and being that are healthy and balanced.

Thresholds (hands-on)

I give credit to my dear friend and colleague, Cathy Gawlick, for teaching me about thresholds, which I have adapted here. Thresholds are a place of pausing and assessing from where we are now to where we are going to. It is a place to pause and to decide how to act.

For example, I was recently reading an article discussing how new lawyers want to dig in and get going on a new project immediately. That makes sense, given the excitement and the adrenaline, but the article talked about needing a plan before getting started, so that you have the bigger picture of where this case is going.

What is missing in these plans, as you may understand by now is how you and your health are included.

You can include many places for health.

In this tool, we pause to think about how we are going to move through this project.

Are we going in a calm, healthy, balanced, and productive way? Or are we proceeding in a way that disregards our own basic health initiatives? How is this occurring?

Quietly reflect and jot down what this might look like.

Learn to stop and take the time to mark these places of entry, because they will, for the most part, determine how you move through the project, and ultimately your life.

For instance, before I crossed the threshold to start writing this book, I marked the moment by remembering my previous book and honoring myself by thanking God for giving me the intellect and the tenacity to move forward in this daunting project.

I also marked the threshold by actively surrounding myself with things that bring me comfort. I am sitting in my favorite writing spot in front of the French windows at my dining room table, with a maple-syrup candle burning, a dog at my feet, a cup of coffee and a bottle of water at my side. That is perfect for me.

Now determine what is perfect for you.

Create it as you step through your threshold.

Journaling (hands-on)

Journaling calms the hectic and sometimes, nonstop conversation in our head.

A great thing about journaling is that you can write what you need down and literally close the book on it.

It will be there tomorrow or later for you.

Journaling can help you remember, create, plan, record or just stop and feel.

Some people like to take a couple of minutes to journal in the morning or in the evening. I like to do both. I especially like to journal during stressful periods of time. Journaling allows me to take care of my emotional self and intellectually process, so that I can "clear room" in my head to take on the next task. Sometimes journaling helps me to keep moving forward with the current task.

Another soothing journaling activity, is to journal a few basic things that you are grateful for, such as coffee, family, friends, etc.

Try journaling something new every day that you are grateful for.

This technique forces you to see what is currently going on in your life that is good and that you sometimes forget about. An example I may include for me might be drinking out of a bright yellow mug that I picked up on a trip to my favorite Italian restaurant, or drinking hot tea on a rainy day.

Think of simple things that you are already doing for yourself. This Tool brings awareness and reinforcement to the positive and healthy behaviors that you are currently engaging in.

Compassion Break (cognitive)

Take a one-minute break.

Stop everything and take a breath, stretch at your desk, and gaze at something in the distance to relax and strengthen your eye muscles.

Have a drink of water.

It is also possible to create a compassion break in a team meeting. It can be done at any time in the group meeting. It seems to be particularly useful at the end of the meeting, where a one-minute timer can be set and people can close their eyes to relax and reinvigorate for the task ahead.

Gifts, Part 2 (hands-on)

Give yourself permission while on your journey at work to give yourself small uplifting gifts every so often.

Try a new, colorful, and fun pen, something that you can use during your day while working or studying that may lighten up your mood.

At my dining-room table, my designated workspace, and at my conference table at work, I have a colored printout of my new mascot, Sydney, my friend's giant yellow parrot with an attitude. I love his look; he is so serious it makes me laugh.

Find special things that only you need to know about and enjoy them while you are working.

This is about creative living and not just enduring.

Ecopsychology (hands-on)

Ecopsychology is the science of letting nature nurture.

When was the last time you walked outside and just listened, smelled, felt, and looked around you?

How could you bring nature to you?

Can you put out a bird feeder? Can you bring a plant inside? Can you bring a plant to work and watch it grow and nurture it? Take some time with the thought, perhaps a bonsai tree?

Several years ago, I had a group of executives who were stressed, anxious, and stuck.

I asked the executives to take care of a bonsai and bring it to work.

They were required to take care of the bonsai for six months.

Now the great thing about a bonsai is that the very concept of it requires slowing down. A bonsai is beautifully decorative, but requires tending over time.

The executives were overly prepared. They were supplied with miniature shears and a miniature watering can as well as a water spritzer and fertilizer. All of this was kept in a tiny box in some remote part of the desk. Everyone agreed to the task and were ready and waiting to get started.

The key word is waiting.

With a bonsai, one must wait and watch. It grows slowly and on its own time, not ours. Some of the people hurt their plant by over-fertilizing or overwatering to get the plant to grow or even blossom.

They were pushing the plant.

Years later some members of the group still had their bonsai. They were more patient with the plant and had learned how to trim it slowly and carefully into the size and shape they wanted. The bonsai is a big-picture plant.

Pop-Up Playtime (hands-on)

Call a local animal shelter and ask if they provide any sort of playtime with puppies or kittens. Many shelters will bring the animals to your location for a fee, which supports the shelters and the animals they house.

Playing with pets has been shown to reduce stress.

Have fun, and who knows, maybe you will find a companion animal to adopt.

Companion animals provide a link outside of us; something other than us and our problems to focus on. Companion animals can be very therapeutic.

But they also require a forever home, and thus a commitment.

Enjoy the fun that only puppies and kittens can provide. It is about fun and frolic, letting go and being care-free.

Do not be surprised if you find yourself laughing out loud. When was the last time that happened?

Animal Companions (hands-on)

Science has demonstrated again and again the physical and mental health benefits of companion animals.

If you do not have a pet, maybe you could help a neighbor or friend. Or go to a dog park and spend time watching dogs play. One or two dogs are sure to come up to you for a pet.

If you do not want to get so close and personal, stop by the humane society or a sanctuary. Check out the fish or the lizards.

I particularly enjoy gazing at the lizards from time to time, and I have thought about adopting two geckos or small lizards for an office terrarium. I like the lizards because first, I have to slow down to see them. I must look carefully in the foliage to find them. Then, interestingly, as I watch and they are so still, I suddenly see them blink. They are amazing little creatures, with their skills at camouflaging into their environments.

When I am watching them and they are watching me, I find myself slowing down and almost giggling to myself about how hectic life can be at times. I also recognize that at this moment in my life, I do not have the time now to care for them, so I only visit.

Find out which animal you would like to visit and enjoy.

Handiwork (hands-on)

Handiwork can be quieting and meditative. It can be anything from beading, knitting, and whittling to making fish lures. Handiwork is work that we do with our hands, and it provides a steady focus, which in turn allows our mind to quiet down.

Handiwork usually does not require intense concentration, and often one can listen to music or watch a movie while creating. You may also find that you are less anxious in these activities, if you do handiwork while participating in them.

Create a list of handiwork ideas and see which one you can begin this week. You may restart an old project or start something new. Enjoy.

Magic Carpet Ride (cognitive)

We all remember the story, a magic carpet that can fly us to magical places.

Let us get on that magic carpet, in our minds.

Let us imagine flying off, away from here.

Feel the soft breeze on your face, feel your hair lift and fly away from your face, and feel your body weight sink into the carpet.

Where are you flying to?

What do you see below you?

What do you see above and all around you?

What do you smell?

What do you hear?

What do you taste if anything?

Stay for a little while on your magic carpet, and if you choose swoop in and out, up and down, through valleys or alleys, wherever your heart desires.

Now come back.

Notice your body. Notice your emotional self.

Take a deep breath and restart your work. You should feel more relaxed and focused. Enjoy your renewed energy and concentration after your short break.

Color Wheel (hands on)

Print out a Color Wheel.

Take a moment to write a feeling on each color as you move through the color wheel.

Which color or colors were most calming?

Which color or colors were most energizing?

Can you incorporate these colors into your day?

Can you wear the color so when you see your image as you pass by a mirror, you will be reminded of the feeling?

If you cannot wear the color, perhaps you can simply keep a small sample of the color on your desk to remind you of feeling states that you enjoy and or want to experience more frequently.

Tuning Fork (cognitive)

We are like tuning forks; we vibrate with invisible energy. Have you ever been feeling fine or neutral and walk into a room with a person or people under stress or distress? We can feel the atmosphere in the room and if we are not aware, we suddenly match our own feeling state with the state of the room.

Recognize your own energy, what you are giving out, and what you are receiving from others. It is true, if we are in a negative state of mind, we start to perceive things in a negative fashion. Just as when we are in a positive energy state, things around us look positive.

Let's try the tool. Wherever you are right now, look at five different objects. Determine something you simply don't like about each object, such as its shape or color.

Now take a breath and close your eyes for just a few seconds. Open your eyes. What do you notice in your body and what do you notice about your emotional state? Now let's look at the same objects, but this time pick out positive qualities. Complete the entire tour of the room with your eyes. Make sure to visit each object.

Now close your eyes and breathe for a couple of seconds. Now open your eyes. What do you notice about your body and your emotional state?

You should have experienced a change in your physical and emotional self. When you were looking for negative things, you may have experienced tightness in your body or holding of your breath and a negative or even angry attitude. When you were looking at things in a positive way, you may have experienced yourself relaxing in your body, letting go, and feeling your emotional state a little more relaxed or lighter.

We have the ability to change our own energy levels and feelings states. In fact, we just did. Every now and then, check yourself and adjust physically and emotionally.

Toybox (hands-on)

A toybox is for fun and to break monotony or a stress cycle. What things can you place in your box that remind you to have fun? What can you do for thirty seconds to a minute that will help?

I love gel pens. How about using a gel pen to take notes or doodle for a while? Or try yo-yos; bubbles; Slime, Silly Putty, Play-Doh, comic books, or a kaleidoscope. You are taking a fun, silly moment to realign.

Our Story (cognitive)

What is your story? We have an ongoing personal dialog with ourselves. This dialog is about value and judgment and determining the next step to take. Sometimes these next steps are based on old, obsolete stories. Are you using any of these obsolete stories in your daily dialog?

What stories are historical and need to be forgotten? Where did they come from, and how old were you when these stories were created? These questions may help you to uncover old stories that are no longer needed but that still impact day to day living.

When under stress, we sometimes revert to the old narratives. They are old and no longer relevant, but we cling to them tenaciously. Watch yourself and check it. You now have new ways of behaving and being that are healthy and balanced.